William Bolcom

T0059220

Let Evening Come

for soprano, viola and piano

CONTENTS

Let Evening Come was recorded by Benita Valente, soprano; Cynthia Raim, piano;
Michael Tree, viola; released on Centaur Records CRC2464.

ISBN 0-634-06582-3

EDWARD B. MARKS MUSIC COMPANY / EXCLUSIVELY DISTRIBUTED BY HAL•LEONARD®

In 1993 I was requested to write a singing duet for Tatiana Troyanos and Benita Valente, two wonderful artists. We discussed possible texts, and then very unexpectedly Tatiana died, a blow to all of us. I was then approached by the sponsors of the commission: Would I write a duo anyway, with Benita Valente, Cynthia Raim as pianist, and Michael Tree as violist, the violist in some way representing the departed Tatiana? The present cantata is the result.

The three poems chosen describe with ever greater acceptance the phenomenon of death. Maya Angelou's poem is still raw with the shock of so many lost artists of the African-American pantheon but observes with an almost journalistic candor the state we, the survivors, pass through after the death of a powerful person. Emily Dickinson's continues in the same dispassionate vein, observation not softening the grief but resolving it through deeper understanding; Jane Kenyon's invites us to contemplate the elegant beauty in death's resolution.

The violist's role did not turn out to be a ghostly recreation of Troyanos' spirit but, perhaps, that of choral commentator on the poems' events. Though each setting is detachable from the other two, the viola-and-piano interlude between the last two poems is not; it serves as gateway to the "coming of evening."

— William Bolcom

Let Evening Come, dedicated to Tatiana Troyanos, was jointly commissioned for Benita Valente by Lincoln Center Productions and by the Gloria Narramore Moody Foundation in memory of Frank McCorkle Moody.

Let Evening Come

Maya Angelou

William Bolcom

1. Ailey, Baldwin, Floyd, Killens, and Mayfield

Strong; moderato, ♩ = **48 or slower** *

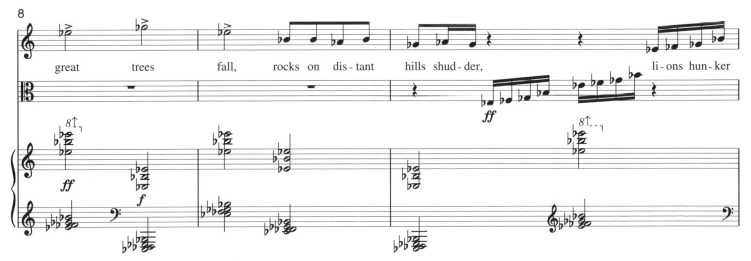

* All metronome markings are approximate.

N. B.: Accidentals apply throughout a beamed group.

down in tall gras - ses, and ev - en el - e - phants lum - ber af - ter safe - ty

When great trees fall _____ in for - ests,

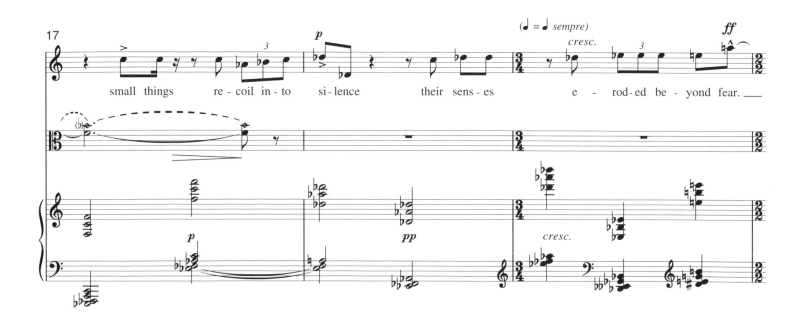

small things re - coil in - to si - lence their sens - es e - rod - ed be - yond fear. ___

When great souls die, the air a-

round us be-comes light, rare, ster-ile. We breathe, brief-ly. Our eyes, brief-ly,

see with a hurt-ful clar-i-ty. Our mem-o-ry, sud-den-ly sharp-ened, ex-am-ines,

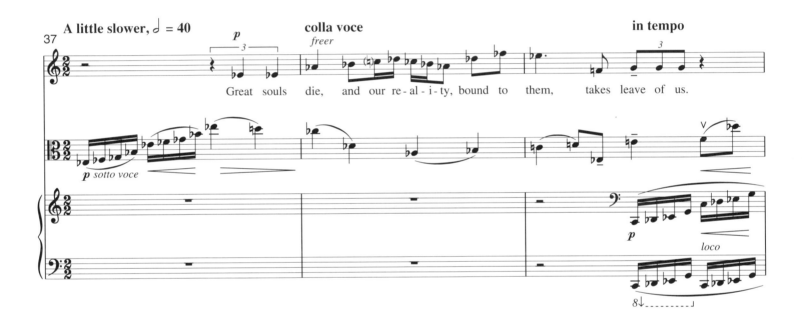

formed and in-formed by their ra-diance, fall a-way. ___ We are not so

much mad-dened as re-duced to the un-ut-ter-a-ble ig-nor-ance of dark, cold

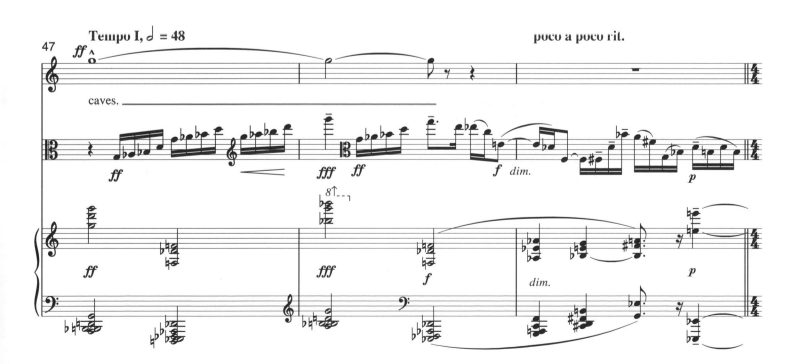

caves. ___

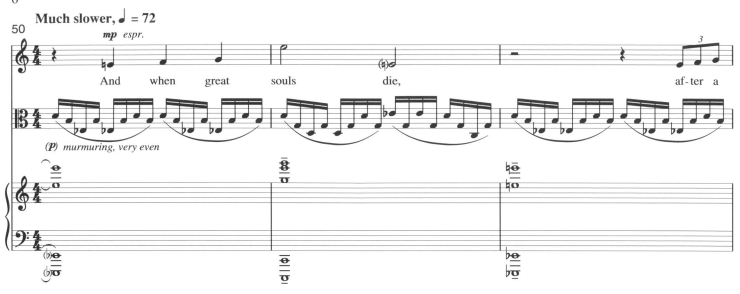

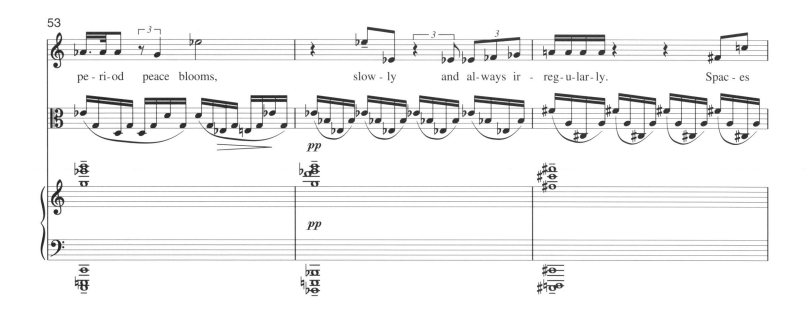

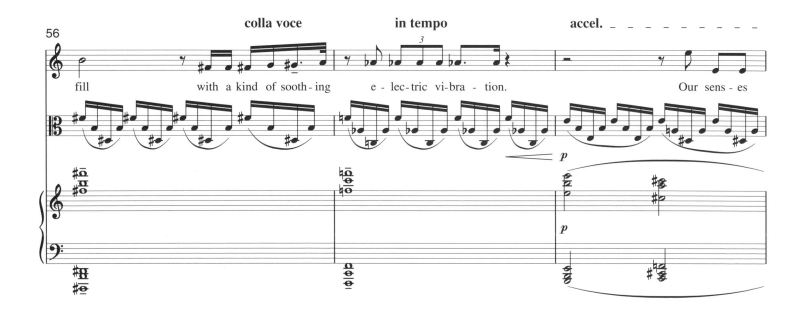

re-stored, nev-er to be the same, whis-per to us. They ex-ist-ed. They ex -

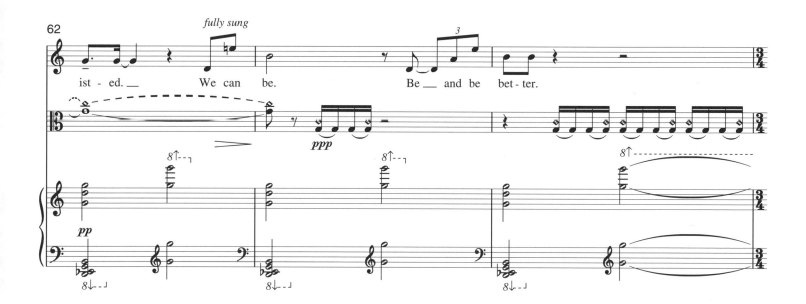

ist - ed. __ We can be. Be __ and be bet-ter.

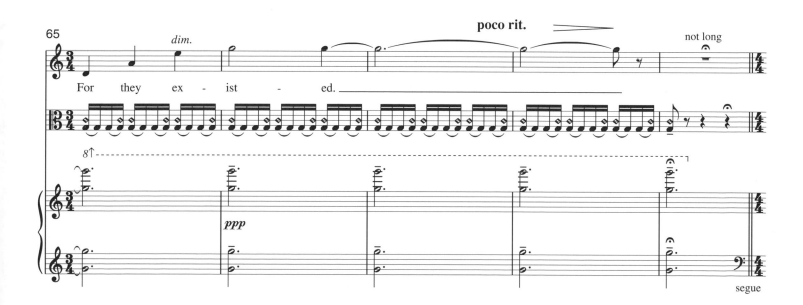

For they ex - ist - ed. _____

2. 'Tis not that Dying hurts us so

Emily Dickinson

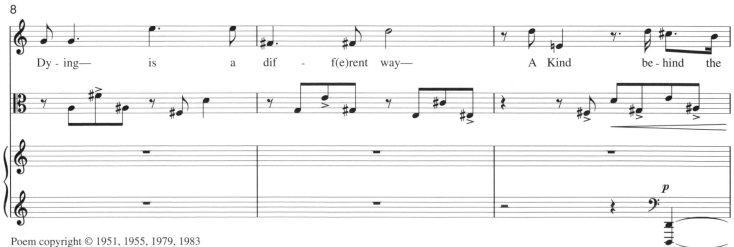

Door—_____ The South - ern Cus - tom—____

____ of the Bird— That ere the Frosts are due—_____

Ac - cepts a bet - ter Lat - i - tude—

We— ___ are the Birds— that stay._____

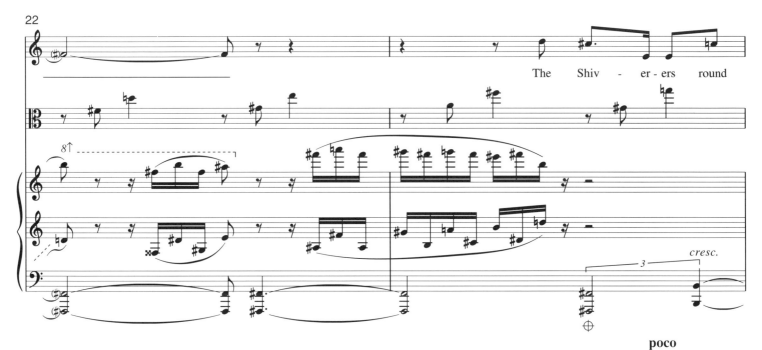

The Shiv - er - ers round

Farm - ers' doors— For whose re - luc - tant Crumb— _____ We stip - u - late—

William Bolcom

Let Evening Come

for soprano, viola and piano

ISBN 0-634-06582-3

EDWARD B. Marks Music Company / EXCLUSIVELY DISTRIBUTED BY HAL•LEONARD®

Viola

Let Evening Come

William Bolcom

1. Ailey, Baldwin, Floyd, Killens, and Mayfield

41

poco allarg. **Tempo I,** ♩ = 48

46

poco a poco rit. **Much slower,** ♩ = 72

49

51

54

colla voce **in tempo**

56

accel. _ _ _ _ _ _ _ _ _ _ _ _ **Tempo I**

58

61

poco rit. not long

66

segue

2. 'Tis not that Dying hurts us so

3. Interlude

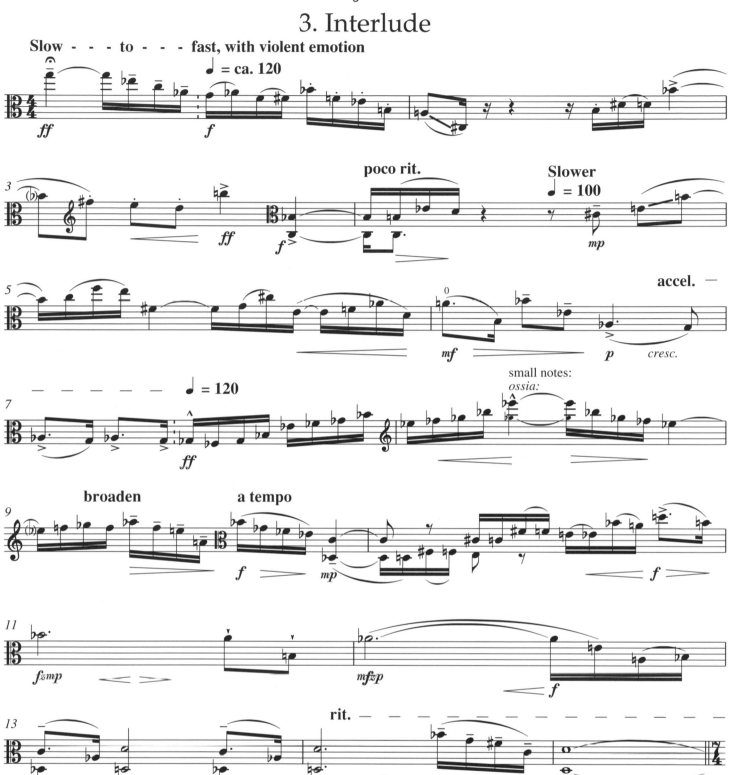

4. Let Evening Come

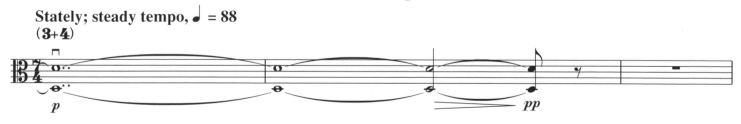

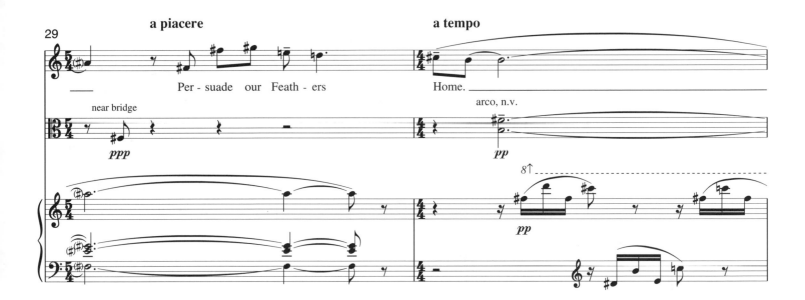

attacca

3. Interlude

Slow - - - - to - - - fast, with violent emotion

𝅘𝅥 = ca. 120

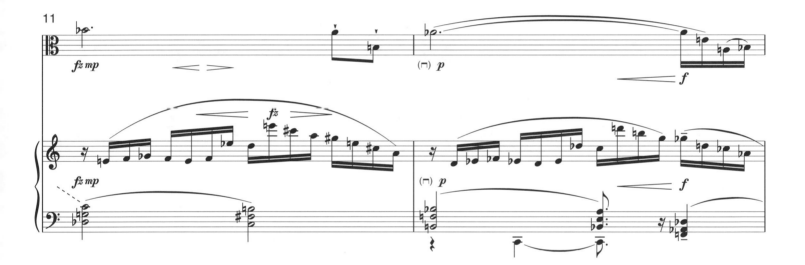

4. Let Evening Come

Jane Kenyon

light _____ of late af - ter - noon _____

shine through chinks in the barn, _____ mov-ing up the

(4+3)

bales as the sun moves down. _____

p

p light

Let the crick - et take up chaf - ing as a wo - man takes up her nee - dles and her

yarn. _____ Let eve - ning come. _____

Let dew col - lect on the hoe a - ban - doned in

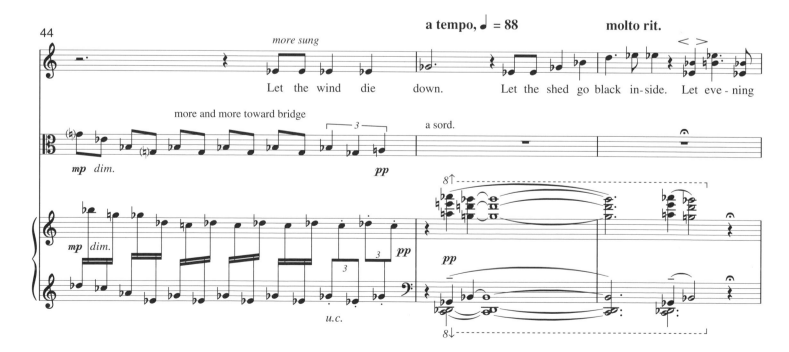

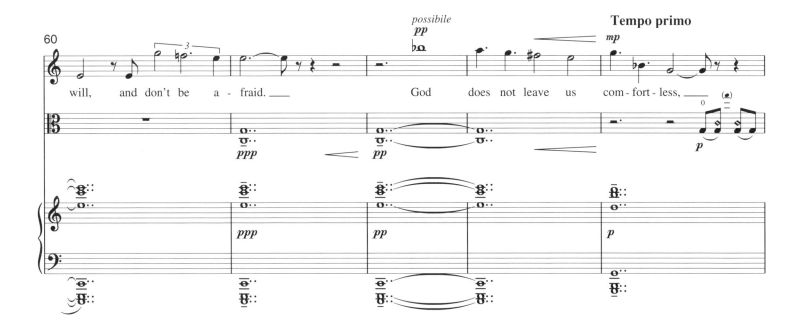

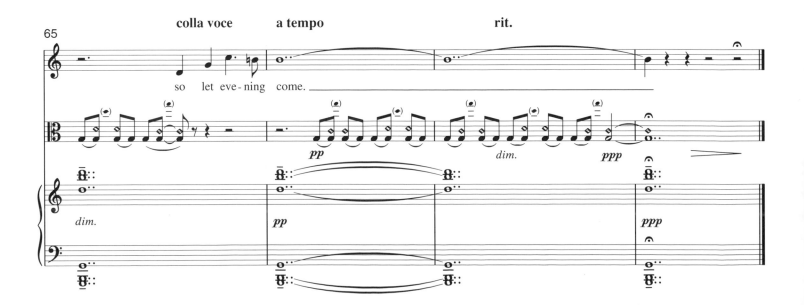